THE POCKET LIBRARY OF GREAT ART

Plate 1. SELF-PORTRAIT. *1652. Oil. Museum, Vienna*

(REMBRANDT HARMENSZ VAN RIJN)

REMBRANDT

(1606 – 1669)

text by

WILHELM KOEHLER

Professor of Fine Arts, Harvard University

With illustrations selected by the Editorial Staff

published by HARRY N. ABRAMS, INC., *in association with* POCKET BOOKS, INC., *New York*

On the cover
detail of SELF-PORTRAIT *(plate 29)*

Plate 2. JEWS IN A SYNAGOGUE. *1648. Etching*
The Metropolitan Museum of Art, New York

Rembrandt

Rembrandt Harmensz van Rijn was born in 1606 at
Leyden, in the small Calvinist republic of the United
Netherlands, which covered approximately the territory
of present-day Holland and numbered barely two million
inhabitants. For twenty-five years the country had pre-
served its independence from absolutist and Catholic
Spain in a precarious struggle demanding heavy sacrifices.
The Twelve Years' Truce, concluded in 1609, changed
the situation entirely. Within a few years the United
Netherlands, with Amsterdam its focal point, has won

a leading position in textile manufacture and international trade and, in fact, is virtually the vital center of European economic life.

Rembrandt's father owns a windmill. The son is determined to become a painter. His earliest dated paintings show that at the age of twenty he has formed independent views about art in general and about his own professional aims as well. He is twenty-five when he moves to Amsterdam where, as the result of rapidly growing prosperity, people make and spend money easily. The young artist at once becomes popular as a portraitist and soon obtains the high distinction of a commission from the political head of the country, Prince Frederick Henry of Orange, to paint a cycle of religious paintings for his private chapel.

So Rembrandt, reared in the quiet, provincial town of Leyden, is drawn into the maelstrom of the great metropolis. He, too, makes and spends money easily. He marries a well-to-do girl, Saskia, in 1634. He frequents public sales of works of art and starts a collection; contracting a heavy mortgage, he goes beyond his means and acquires a stately house in the center of the city. People begin to gossip and to accuse him of squandering the inheritance of his wife through extravagance and display. In 1642 Saskia dies. Rembrandt and his infant son, Titus, are left alone. A few years later Rembrandt takes Hendrickje Stoffels into his house, outraging the Calvinist righteousness of his fellow citizens. Many doubtless think that it serves him right when, after his clumsy attempts to proclaim his social status as an independent artist in the midst of prosperous businessmen, his financial difficulties multiply, while his popularity as a portraitist rapidly declines and the occasional sale of a painting or etching remains his only, and very insecure, source of subsistence. Long, hard years of struggle with adversity

Plate 3. BEGGARS RECEIVING ALMS. *1648. Etching*
Museum of Fine Arts, Boston

Plate 4. CHRIST HEALING THE SICK (THE "HUNDRED GUILDER PRINT")

About 1649. Etching. The Metropolitan Museum of Art, New York

follow. The end is financial collapse and bankruptcy—which means that, in the eyes of Amsterdam mercantile society, he is stigmatized as a sort of outcast.

Now the ambitious dreams of youth have definitely foundered. In the summer of 1656 the authorities are busy making an inventory of Rembrandt's possessions, including his house, his collections, and his household goods, which are subsequently sold in lots by public auction. The aging artist—penniless, his creditors watching out for any income they can lay hands upon—must submit to being appointed an employee of the firm of Titus and Hendrickje, dealers in art; and in 1660 he moves out to the poorest quarter of the city.

Two great commissions come his way during these last years: for the Clothmakers' Guild he paints a group portrait of their governing board, famous as *The Syndics* or *Staalmeesters,* and for a wall of the new City Hall, the pride of wealthy Amsterdam, now in the heyday of its prosperity after the close of the Thirty Years' War, he paints a huge canvas representing a legendary event in the ancient history of Holland, the Conspiracy of the Batavians. This painting was installed in 1661, but for unknown reasons it was returned to Rembrandt in the following year and replaced by the thoroughly insignificant work of a second-rate artist. We can only guess how deeply Rembrandt must have felt this humiliation after all his previous trials and disappointments. Was it not more than a human being could be expected to bear? But Fate had still other blows in store for him. The same year that the authorities of the city rejected one of his greatest works, only a fragment of which was saved for posterity, his faithful helper, Hendrickje Stoffels, passed away, and in 1668 his son died at the age of twenty-seven.

As his popularity declined and his financial difficulties increased Rembrandt secluded himself more and more

Plate 5. THE SACRIFICE OF ABRAHAM. *1655. Etching*
The Metropolitan Museum of Art, New York

from the robust and busy world around him. Few people seem to have stayed by him in the tribulations of his last years. He must have been a very lonely man, all but forgotten by his fellow citizens, when he closed his eyes forever in 1669, a year after the death of his son.

This is the sad story of Rembrandt's life. Who will venture to say what part of this misery was his own fault, what part was the result of adversity from without? To us, today, he speaks through his work alone, and it is a powerful and clear voice that speaks.

If a distinction may be made between the physical and the spiritual in man, Rembrandt in his Leyden years tends to concentrate one-sidedly on the spiritual. In the first ten years in Amsterdam, interest in the physical predominates. Then follows a gradual integration of the two elements, until at last the artist has at his command a visual language which enables him to proclaim the spiritual in man with a power and intensity never before attained in painting.

Almost any group of Rembrandt's works, however much chosen at random, offers proof of the eloquence with which he conveyed the expressive content of his theme. In a brief study such as this it is through examining the content, rather than through attempting to analyze the formal and technical devices which he employed, that we shall arrive most directly at the response the artist hoped we would have to what he is trying to say.

Plate 6. WOMAN AT THE BATH. *1648. Etching*
The Metropolitan Museum of Art, New York

Plate 7. THE THREE TREES. *1643. Etching*

The Metropolitan Museum of Art, New York

Plate 8. PORTRAIT OF JAN LUTMA. *1656. Etching*
The Metropolitan Museum of Art, New York

COLOR PLATES

PLATE 9

Painted about 1628

PRESENTATION IN THE TEMPLE

Kunsthalle, Hamburg

21¾ x 17⅜"

When Rembrandt painted this picture, at about the age of twenty-two, he was obviously not yet master of the correct proportioning and rendering of the human figure, and he still employed compositional devices which he had learned from his teachers. This matters but little, however, when weighed against the originality of his interpretation of the Biblical story. No one had previously shown the Presentation scene as centering in the emotional experience of the Virgin. The aged Simeon is addressing her; she looks toward the Child whom Simeon holds in his arms. Her clasped hands and wide-eyed gaze allow us to share the inner struggle between her feelings as a mother and her realization that this, her child, is a Divine Being, whose earthly destiny is now revealed to her.

It is the inner relation between mother and child that forms the compelling theme of the painting. Everything else is mere accompaniment: Simeon's gesture, the kneeling figure of Joseph, and Anna starting back in awe, her silhouette holding the whole group together and relating it to the background details of the Temple architecture.

PLATE 10

Painted about 1629/30

THE RAISING OF LAZARUS

By Courtesy of the Rijksmuseum, Amsterdam

37½ x 32⅜"

Though not more than a year or two later than the *Presentation in the Temple* (plate 9), the *Lazarus* shows distinct progress. The young artist has gained in knowledge of the human figure and he now handles the compositional device of the triangle in a manner entirely his own.

In abrupt ascent, the figures at the left build toward a summit. The eye is led upward from the woman shrinking back in fear to the commanding gesture of Christ, which dominates the whole painting. In contrast to this vertical emphasis comes the forward thrust of the figures on either side of Christ. These lateral figures provide a connecting link with the body of Lazarus, which occupies the lower right corner of the triangle. Lazarus is manifestly not raising himself; he is being drawn upward by Christ's lifted arm.

A side light sharply intensifies the expressive content of movements and gestures without wholly dispelling the darkness of the cave. Through use of this pervading twilight as medium Christ's supernatural power is made believable, and the whole painting becomes a convincing evocation of the greatest of all miracles: the awakening of man from the dead.

PLATE II

Painted in 1637

THE ANGEL LEAVING TOBIAS
AND HIS FAMILY

The Louvre, Paris

26¾ x 20½"

In the biblical narrative, God has rewarded the aged
Tobias for his faith by sending the angel Raphael who
cures the old man's blindness and finds wealth and a
wife for his son. Raphael, taking leave of the family,
reveals himself as an angel, sent by God, "and having
said that he vanished out of their sight." It is this moment of climax that Rembrandt has chosen to illustrate.

Everything in this early work is momentary and tran-
sitory. There is no suggestion in the text of the
dramatic suddenness with which, in the painting, the
youth, transformed into a winged angel, starts up into
sudden flight and disappears in the blinding light that
breaks through the dark clouds in front of the house.
This dramatic interpretation contrasts singularly with
the epic leisure of the text which, however, Rembrandt
follows closely in other respects. What we learn of each
person's character is admirably summed up in the action of the figures: the pious shyness of the old man,
who does not dare to watch the miracle happen; the
terror and lack of confidence of his wife, who lets the
stick slip from her hands; the secure faith of the young
couple who look up more in awe than in fear, while
their hands instinctively join in prayer.

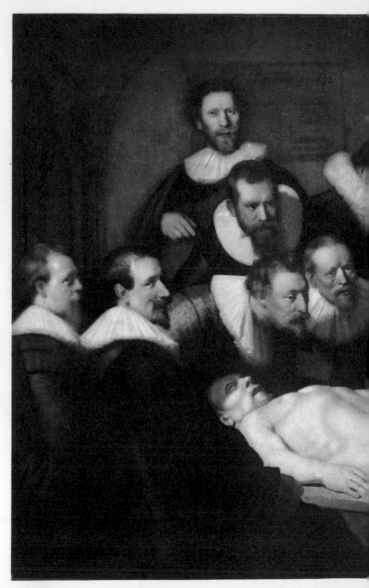

Plate 12. THE ANATOMY LESSON OF DR. TULP *(commentary follows col*

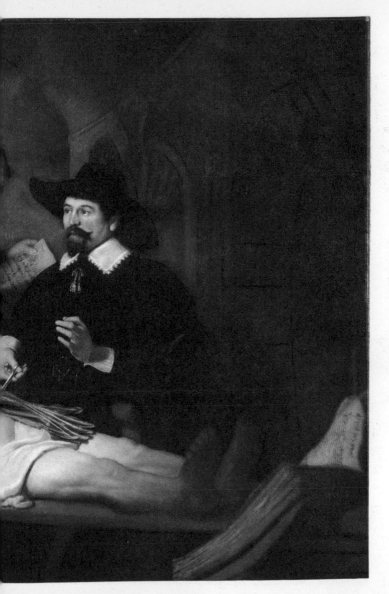

section). See plates 13 & 14 following

Plate 15. CHRIST AT EMMAUS *(detail of plate 30).*

Commentary follows color plate section

portion of plate 16 (open page opposite)

PLATE 16

Painted in 1638

SAMSON'S WEDDING FEAST

State Gallery, Dresden

49⅝ x 68⅞"

A beam of light singles out two figures: the woman in the center and the tall man turning away from her. The composition, surpassing in subtle skill anything that Rembrandt had achieved in his earlier work, suggests a motion that runs from the left to the right, ending in the telling gesture of the man's hands.

This man is Samson, the indomitable hero, endowed with superhuman strength, who is shown presenting his insoluble riddle to the group of attentively listening Philistines: "Out of the eater came forth meat; and out of the strong came forth sweetness" (Judges, XIV, 14). The woman in the center, an enigmatic expression on her face, is the bride who subsequently betrays Samson after extorting from him the solution to the riddle. Gathered around the table are the wedding guests, talking, laughing, making love—an assortment of sinister types, each caught in the moment of action or with the particular expression on his face which most fully reveals his baser instincts.

PLATE 17

Painted in 1652

AN OLD MAN IN THOUGHT

The Devonshire Collection (Reproduced by Permission of the Trustees of the Chatsworth Settlement)

44½ x 35"

Rembrandt's technique and style are changing in the years after 1650. He now begins to apply the color to the canvas with broad strokes of the brush; instead of blending many colors into subdued harmonies in dim light, he sometimes makes use of one strong color accent and a very bright light.

Our painting is quite possibly merely the study of a model whom the artist has costumed in a rich robe and posed where a beam of strong light would bring out the whole gamut of color. Rembrandt had painted studies after nature such as this in his earlier years, when his approach and his aims were different. He takes them up again now as new aspects of the world around him appeal to his senses and challenge his imagination. It is not to paintings of this type that one will look for a full measure of the artist's creative possibilities; rather, they are in the nature of exercises. They represent stepping stones which enabled Rembrandt to rise to the heights of the great masterpieces of his last years.

PLATE 18

Painted in 1654

A WOMAN BATHING

National Gallery, London

24 x 17¾"

Rembrandt shows here an untroubled surrender to visual impressions rare among his paintings. Usually, when his eyes become fascinated with some object or figure of the moment, he is satisfied with recording it in a drawing, which may or may not later be used for an etching. His remarkable print of *The Golf Player* (plate 31), for example, dating from the same year as this painting, actually anticipates the Impressionist tendencies of the nineteenth century in its choice of subject matter and its bold handling of light effects.

Our painting, however, can make no such claim. The carefully arranged background of draperies is a contemporary note, and the color scheme has in it nothing of nineteenth-century analytical procedure. But even more basic is the difference in the artist's attitude toward his subject. The bather is not painted with the cool detachment of the Impressionist creed; her features are unmistakably those of Hendrickje Stoffels, and this study from nature is thus in all probability an intimate portrait—as intimate as Rubens' famous portrait of his wife covering her nude body with a fur coat.

Plate 19. THE NIGHT WATCH (commentary follows color plate sectio

PLATE 20

Painted in 1654

BATHSHEBA

The Louvre, Paris

55⅛ x 55⅛"

Hendrickje served as model for this large painting as well as for the small *Woman Bathing* (plate 18), but the mode of representation is strikingly different. In the smaller painting, the rapid brush strokes seem hardly able to keep up with the intensity and fascination of the visual perception. In the *Bathsheba,* the nude body as well as the accessories are rendered with great care, the forms being built up by deliberate brushwork, with gradual transitions of tone.

The striking difference in style can be accounted for by the difference of purpose. One painting is a study of nature containing no narrative element. The other represents the biblical story of the beautiful Bathsheba whom David had desired and summoned to him. The letter held by the woman in the painting identified her to Rembrandt's contemporaries. What distinguishes Rembrandt's treatment of the popular theme is that he has not only represented Bathsheba as a woman "very beautiful to look upon," but he has allowed us to participate in her inner struggle between fidelity to her husband and obedience to the king. The nude body, in all its splendor, leads our eyes up to the head and to the face, heavy with deep emotions which anyone familiar with the story could not fail to grasp.

portion of plate 21 (open page opposite)

PLATE 23

Painted about 1658

PORTRAIT OF TITUS

Museum, Vienna

27¾ x 25¼"

The portraits of Titus and Hendrickje (next plate) are related to each other in subject matter as well as in style. Titus, Saskia's only surviving child, was about seventeen and Hendrickje about thirty-two when their likenesses were painted: both portraits, then, postdate Rembrandt's financial ruin, and the fact that we meet in them the two human beings who shared with him the hardships of the following years lends them a special poignancy from the biographical point of view.

In both portraits the sitter seems to be enveloped in a mysterious, luminous sphere, woven of color and light, which relates them not only to the surrounding space but to us as well. We feel that we are in direct and curiously intimate contact with them since their painted images convey to us much more than a convincing reflection of external appearances.

Titus, relaxed in his chair, is absorbed in his reading. Accents of color and light cause our eyes to vacillate between face and book. We are made to share in his absorption as though we were looking over his shoulder and reading, and thus the contact with him is established.

PLATE 24

Painted about 1659

HENDRICKJE STOFFELS

Kaiser Friedrich Museum, Berlin

34 x 26"

With Hendrickje we communicate still more directly than with Titus (previous plate). She looks out at us from the simplest of settings—a window frame against which she is leaning. Her brown eyes meet our own with a gentle candor to which we instantly respond. We are in contact with a distinct personality, whose charm is not only expressed in subtle details of facial expression, but diffused through the characteristic pose of the body as well.

Rembrandt painted several portraits of Hendrickje during the years preceding her death in 1662. He has shown her in different moods and different positions—in the last likeness of all with an expression of profound sadness. But beneath the changing states of mind appear certain invariable basic traits which Rembrandt evidently wanted to record. Our painting may well reflect more clearly than any other the rare capacity for devotion and self-denial suggested by the little that we actually know of Hendrickje.

portion of plate 25 (open page opposite)

PLATE 25

Painted in 1662

THE BOARD OF THE CLOTHMAKERS' GUILD

("The Syndics")

Rijksmuseum, Amsterdam

72⅛ x 107⅛"

Rembrandt here takes us into a meeting of the Guild. We sit in the assembly facing the officers. Some disagreement must have been voiced from the floor. The chairman in the center has just given his answer, pointing at the records in front of him; his neighbor to the right has checked the correctness of his statement and now looks intently, as do the other three officers, in the direction of the opponents.

One thought is in the minds of the six men: the point raised by the other side. Shared responsibility draws the group together, but does not efface the differences between personalities. On the contrary, the character and temperament of each man are laid bare by his reactions to the incident. Posture, action, the fleeting reflection of emotions in the faces are so eloquent that we actually seem to be looking into the minds of these Amsterdam businessmen who are so strikingly recreated on the canvas, with all the characteristic details of their physical appearance, that they sparkle with life and actuality.

portion of plate 26 (open page opposite)

Painted about 1667-69

FAMILY PORTRAIT

Herzog Anton Ulrich Museum, Brunswick

49¾ x 65⅞"

In the last years of Rembrandt's life, to which the *Family Portrait* belongs, he had at his command a visual language that in its infinite tenderness and extraordinary power imparts to every work the character of a personal confession.

Even the best reproduction can suggest only faintly the enchantment of this painting. The colors seem to ripple over the surface. They shimmer and glow in multiple refraction against the mysterious dusk of the shadows. The solid forms are not clearly defined in relation to the surrounding space; they decrease in density toward the surface and seem to be on the point of dissolving.

Clothing, body, and face seem to have been fused into one strangely immaterial, intangible substance in which the physical and psychic beings are brought to an unexampled degree of interpenetration. All external appearances are made to subserve this content. It not only completely fills the figure, but radiates from it, and endows it with so persuasive and heightened a reality that we all but sense its palpable nearness. Whereas in earlier paintings it is often the aggressive power of the intellectual alertness and energy that most compels us, in the *Family Portrait* our contact with the figures is established through this vibrating current of life alone.

PLATE 27

Painted in 1659

MOSES SHOWING THE TABLES OF THE LAW

Kaiser Friedrich Museum, Berlin

66½ x 54"

According to the Book of Exodus, the ten command-
ments were given twice to Moses on Mount Sinai. The
first time they were "graven upon the tables" of stone
by Jehovah himself, but Moses broke the tables when
he came down from the mountain and found the
Israelites worshipping the golden calf. The second time,
Moses wrote down God's words himself, and "it came
to pass, when Moses came down from Mount Sinai
with the two tables of testimony in his hand that Moses
knew not that his face shone" (Exodus, XXXIV, 29).

The second return from Sinai, not the breaking of the
tables, is the subject of Rembrandt's painting. What
remains to us is only a fragment of a much larger
canvas that was to have decorated a room in the City
Hall of Amsterdam but was not accepted by the authorities, who preferred instead a representation of the same
subject by one of Rembrandt's former pupils. Nothing
is known about the original composition, of which the
figure of Moses must have been the central part.

PLATE 28

Painted in 1661

MARGARETHA DE GEER

National Gallery, London

30 x 25⅜"

Rembrandt painted Margaretha and her husband, the merchant Jacob Trip of Dordrecht, in two more formal and much larger portraits, at about the same time as the one illustrated here. If not actually a study for the larger painting, it is distinguished by a directness and freshness that give it a particular charm, though it can hardly compete in significance with other late works.

The hair has not lost its youthful color. The glance of the dark eyes, contrasting with the ruddy complexion of the face, is still alive with vigor. Only the sunken temples and the receding corners of the mouth betray the age of Margaretha de Geer, who was seventy-eight years old when Rembrandt painted her. The huge starched frill so familiar in portraits of an earlier generation had long been out of fashion by 1661. The painter manifestly welcomed its reappearance; to him the variety of whites, the stiffness of the transparent material, and the intricate pattern of the folds afforded a wonderful foil for the form, modeling, and color of the head.

PLATE 29

Painted between 1660 and 1665

SELF-PORTRAIT

Kenwood House, London

44⅞ x 38⅛"

If we wish to meet Rembrandt the human being, we must turn to the numerous self-portraits in which he has given us a continuous autobiography covering his life from the age of twenty to the time of his death at the age of sixty-three. No other artist has painted himself so often and probably no other artist has been so candid a reporter of his own image.

Rembrandt may have been approaching his sixties when he painted the portrait reproduced here. The artist has interrupted work for a moment and has turned toward the mirror, planning to set down on the canvas what he sees. He does not spare himself in his portrayal, but shows without concealment the aging features, the sagging cheeks, and heavy chin. The forms of the body are only summarily indicated; there is nothing to hinder the eye from traveling directly upward to the face, and to the dark eyes which meet our own with the open and steadfast gaze of a man whose energies have not been broken by the vicissitudes of his life.

Painted in 1632

THE ANATOMY LESSON OF DR. TULP

Mauritshuis, The Hague

65 x 86½"

The painting records an event unusual for Rembrandt's day: Dr. Tulp, the well-known Amsterdam surgeon, is demonstrating to a group of colleagues—probably the board of directors of the guild—the actual dissection of a human corpse. That the physicians, in order to commemorate this rare performance, gave their commission to the young painter who only recently had moved from Leyden to Amsterdam, shows how quickly Rembrandt must have established his reputation.

The task of assembling eight portraits on a single canvas was a challenging test. In the religious paintings of the Leyden years Rembrandt had developed his method of constructing groups of small figures, but now the figures were to be of life size, and to portray individuals.

Though each of the heads is rendered with utmost care and clarity—each apparently a faithful likeness—the eyes are in every case the most significant feature. Their gaze has a shared intensity which makes external differences between the individuals seem of little importance: the body is merely the shell in which the psychic energies are lodged.

The pyramidal composition has as its sole function to contain the accumulated tension and channel its impact in the desired direction.

Painted in 1642

THE NIGHT WATCH

Rijksmuseum, Amsterdam

11' 11¾" x 14' 4½"

Following an old Dutch custom, a company of the Civil Guard of Amsterdam commissioned Rembrandt in 1642 to paint the portraits of its members on a huge canvas to be placed in its assembly hall. Breaking with the traditional scheme of a single or double row of standing figures, facing the spectator, the young artist has shown the guards at a moment of striking activity, each making his preparations to fall in at the expected command. Since the figures are of life-size, an overwhelming effect is produced by the outward thrust of the central group as it streams forward in wedge-shaped formation from the dark doorway.

The contrast with the flanking groups and with figures moving in opposite directions, the diagonals furnished by standard, muskets, halberds, and pikes, and the distribution of colors intensify the impression of forward momentum which centers in the outstretched right arm of the captain.

The Night Watch is a recapitulation of the ideals of Rembrandt's first ten Amsterdam years, and is the last painting in which he strives for brilliant external effects. From now on he sets himself the aim of recreating in visual terms the intangible essence of man, his inner life.

PLATE 30

(see also detail, color plate 15)

Painted in 1648

CHRIST
AT EMMAUS

The Louvre, Paris
26¾ x 25⅝"

In the village inn at Emmaus, two of Christ's disciples are seated at supper with the stranger who had joined them as they walked away from Jerusalem after the discovery of the empty tomb. The innkeeper may feel that something unusual is happening, as shown by the reverence with which he approaches the guests—but he cannot know. Doubt, questioning, awe mingle in the disciple on the right upon whom the revelation is dawning. It has already taken hold of the other; he knows who the stranger is from whose head a magic light begins to radiate. Christ in the center, his raised eyes reaching out into another world, breaks the bread. "And their eyes were opened, and they knew him."

We must be willing to listen to a delicate music of inner voices if we are to participate in the dramatic tension vibrating between the Risen Christ and the human beings in their struggle between faith and doubt.

Plate 31. THE GOLF PLAYER. *1654. Etching. The Metropolitan Museum of Art, New York*

Plate 32. FAUST IN HIS STUDY. *1652. Etching*
The Metropolitan Museum of Art, New York

Plate 33. THE DESCENT FROM THE CROSS. *1654. Etching*
The Metropolitan Museum of Art, New York

Plate 34. THE THREE CROSSES. *1653. Etching*

The Metropolitan Museum of Art, New York

Plate 35. CHRIST PRESENTED TO THE PEOPLE. *1644. Etching*

The Metropolitan Museum of Art, New York

Plate 36. ST. PETER AND ST. JOHN AT THE BEAUTIFUL GATE
1648/49. Drawing. The Metropolitan Museum of Art

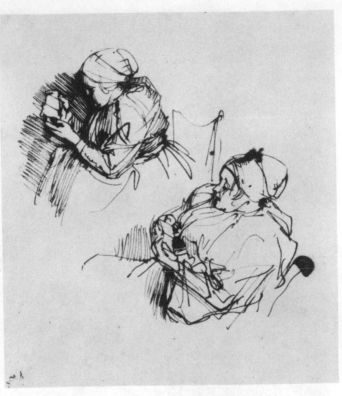

Plate 37. TWO STUDIES OF A WOMAN READING
1633/34. *Drawing. The Metropolitan Museum of Art*

Plate 38. CHRIST PREACHING ("LA PETITE TOMBE")

About 1652. Etching. The Metropolitan Museum of Art

BIOGRAPHICAL NOTES

1606   Rembrandt Harmensz van Rijn born at Leyden, July 15, the son of a miller.

1613–20   Studies in Leyden at the Latin School and for a few months at the University.

1620–25   Studies painting in Leyden and then for six months with Pieter Lastman in Amsterdam.

1625–26   Returns to Leyden; earliest dated work.

1632   Moves from Leyden to Amsterdam. Receives many commissions; growing fame and wealth.

1634   Marries the patrician Saskia van Uylenburgh.

1639   Buys a large house; lives extravagantly.

1641   Birth of his son Titus.

1642   Death of Saskia. Paints *The Night Watch*.

about 1645   Hendrickje Stoffels enters his household.

1656–60   Bankruptcy; sale of his house and auctions of his household property; moves to the poorest quarter of Amsterdam.

1662   Death of Hendrickje.

1668   Death of Titus.

1669   Rembrandt dies in Amsterdam, October 4.

CHANGING VIEWS OF REMBRANDT

Roger de Piles, 1706: "He has sometimes enriched the poverty of his subjects by a happy motion of his genius, but having no certain knowledge of beautiful proportion, he easily relapsed into the bad taste to which he had accustomed himself."

Arnold Houbraken, 1718: "Rembrandt would not be bound by any rúles made by others and not even follow the exalted examples of those who through their rendering of beauty had prepared themselves for eternal fame."

Jean Auguste Dominique Ingres, 1821: "Let us not admire Rembrandt and the others through thick and thin; let us not compare them, either the men or their art, to the divine Raphael and the Italian school: that would be blaspheming."

Eugène Delacroix, 1851: "It may sound like blasphemy, but people will perhaps discover one day that Rembrandt was as great a painter as Raphael."

Eugène Fromentin, 1876: ". . . this so-called materialist, this *trivial, ugly* man was a pure spiritualist . . . If we take him thus, Rembrandt is quite explained—his life, his work, his tendencies, his conceptions, his poetry, his method, his processes, even to the varnish of his paint, which is nothing but a daring and a carefully sought-out spiritualization of the material elements of his craft."

Vincent van Gogh, 1888: "And so Rembrandt has alone or almost alone among painters, that tenderness in the gaze . . . that heartbroken tenderness, that glimpse of a superhuman infinite that seems so natural there."

SOME OTHER BOOKS
ABOUT REMBRANDT

Otto Benesch. *Rembrandt: Selected Drawings*. Two vols. New York, Oxford University Press, 1947

Abraham Bredius. *The Paintings of Rembrandt*. New York, Oxford University Press, 1942

Arthur M. Hind. *A Catalogue of Rembrandt's Etchings*. Two vols. London, Methuen, 1923 (Chronologically arranged and completely illustrated)

Ludwig Münz. *Rembrandt's Etchings*. Two vols. New York, Garden City, 1953 (A critical catalogue)

Jakob Rosenberg. *Rembrandt*. Two vols. Cambridge, Harvard University Press, 1948 (Text and illustrations)

ACKNOWLEDGMENTS

In a book of art, it seems particularly fitting to acknowledge the work of craftsmen who contribute to its making. The color plates were made by Litho-Art, Inc., New York. The lithography is from the presses of The Meehan-Tooker Co., Inc., New York and the binding has been done by F. M. Charlton Co., New York. The paper was made by P. H. Glatfelter Co., Spring Grove, Pa. Our deepest indebtedness is to the museums, galleries, and private collectors who graciously permitted the reproduction of their paintings, drawings, and sculpture.